THE BIG MOSQUE OF MERCY

THE BIG MOSQUE OF MERCY

CHRIS ELLERY

INK
BRUSH
PRESS

Library of Congress Control Number: 2009938159
ISBN 9780982440544

Manufactured in the United States of America
Ink Brush Press
www.inkbrushpress.com
Temple, Texas

Acknowledgments

The author acknowledges with sincere thanks the editors and staff of those publications in which some of these poems originally appeared:

2009 Texas Poetry Calendar: "The Ripe and the Unripe Fruit"
ASU Magazine: "Border Crossing"
descant: "Nearest the Mosque"; "To Those Who Would Kill Me Because I'm American"; "Bimaristan Arghun"
Lilliput Review: "Horizon"
Mizna: "Excursion in Syrian Mesopotamia"; "Man with No Legs"; "After Dinner at Dr. Zafari's House"
Muse²: "The Cedars"
Paterson Literary Review: "A Eucharist at the Canary Hotel"
Rock & Sling: "Meat Market in Aleppo"
Texas Observer: "Defection"

An early version of "Summit" appeared in *As-Salamu Alaykum*, the newsletter of the Muslim Peace Fellowship.

"Bimaristan Arghun" received the 2005 Betsy Colquitt Award from *descant*.

"A Eucharist at the Canary Hotel" received an honorable mention in the 2007 Allen Ginsberg Poetry Awards, sponsored by the Poetry Center at Passaic County Community College, Paterson, NJ.

"The Ripe and the Unripe Fruit" received Third Place in the *2009 Texas Poetry Calendar* Awards.

Some of these poems originally appeared in the collection *All This Light We Live In*. The author is grateful to Panther Creek Press for permission to republish.

This book was made possible by a Fulbright Grant from the Council for the International Exchange of Scholars and by a Faculty Development and Enrichment Grant from Angelo State University.

Shukran kitir to the students, faculty, staff, and administration of the University of Aleppo and to all my friends and fellow travelers in Syria.

بسم الله الرحمن الرحيم

for all servants and seekers, friends of the One,
Who bears the most beautiful names

I laugh when I hear that the fish in the water is thirsty.

You don't grasp the fact that what is most alive of all
is inside your own house.

Kabir

Contents

MIHRAB: QIBLA

IWAN: LEAVING

GLOSSARY

Prologue: Rule for Travel

I have a rule for traveling: *Unpack before leaving.*
Unpack assumptions.
Unpack expectations.
Jettison prejudice.

This is baggage that will weigh you down, trunks that don't load well on the slender boats you must sometimes go on. Too heavy for horses, camels, even elephants. They take up space that you need for essentials: curiosity, self-knowledge, love. These don't weigh anything. That's good because sometimes a donkey or even your own two feet are the only way to get you there.

Go empty.

Expectation blinds the sight-seer to the unexpected. You will seek out what you expect. In Deir Sobat, the tourists were viewing the ruins of a chapel described in the guide book. I was talking to a club-footed boy in a tree. What are ruins, broken stones and rubble, compared to a grinning boy?

Assumption closes doors, hangs signs that say DO NOT OPEN. I heard someone say, upon seeing my friend in the tree, "That boy is a dirty beggar." But he asked me for nothing; instead, he picked and gave me the sweetest orange I have ever tasted.

Prejudice is a fence around the heart. Perhaps it keeps out wolves, but it keeps out friends as well. There is no gate on prejudice. Those who erect such a fence find themselves outside the walls of whatever they hoped to protect. The boy in the tree was not like me, but he called me "uncle." How will the world be worse if I call him "*ibn*"?

Prejudice is like adding gravel to your food.

Prejudice blows up the only bridge that gets you where you need to go.

Those who take along their prejudices, assumptions, expectations are packing for comfort. I can be comfortable at home—no need to travel. Comfort leaves no room in the lifeboat. Someone has to drown.

So I have a rule for traveling: Unpack before leaving.

Tomorrow, today, NOW—this is my time of departure. I am leaving on the journey of the rest of my life.

The trip won't be very long.

The rule applies.

I must travel light.

MINARET

The Large Mosque of Mercy

Jaami' ar-Rahman
like Disneyland
glows in the dark
tip-topped with one red spark
two crescents like forks
turned up on the tops
of its high minarets
as though to spear stars
or the falling *Shaitan*

Evening of Light

The *muezzin*'s call from the minaret of Mercy
bids swarming Aleppo to come to prayers,
come, all Halab, to the best of deeds.
The bee-like taxis drop
their fares. The merchants' wares
line the crowded lanes—
fustuq, textile, mobile, meat.
Mosque after mosque begins to blare
the greatness of God. The voice of Mercy
thrills the air, loud but ignored
like the insistent, futile horns of cars,
diesel belching of bus and truck,
jack-hammer building and demolition.

Deep in old Aleppo, deep in time,
at the foot of age-battered Citadel,
Mercy settles like light, like pollen on dirty streets,
settles on the bastions and in the keep,
drifts and settles in the deepest recess of the covered bazaar.
Mercy on shoulders,
Mercy on feet.
Mercy on those who joke and brag.
Mercy on all who sell and shop.
Mercy on tourists, guides, and police.
Mercy on the children in rags.
Mercy in the stench and perfume.
Mercy on the gleaming souvenirs.
Mercy filling the copper pots.
Mercy on neon minarets.
Mercy in the waters of the public baths.
Mercy on the offal of slaughtered lamb.

Ahmed says everyone wears a mask.
People say yes and then do no.
Ghias peacefully smokes and nods.
We are three in our sleeveless shirts in the heat,
refreshed and cool from cold water baths,
rinsed of excuses and every pretense,
savoring melon and confession to pass the day.
The breeze stirs, and Mercy
lights our faces like the setting sun.

Bayyada, some of my students say,
is a region of grease and common folk.
Why would you live there, sir? they ask.
I walk from my house to Bab al Hadid.
In the woodshops and smithies
the common folk make axes, shovels, rakes, all
the implements that make this country,
forges lit since ages past.
                              Around the corner
from the ancient gate
garages and tire shops, lumber, tools,
markets of produce and laurel soap,
donkey-drawn carts with loads of junk,
fleeces bagged and loaded on trucks.
And on their way to *masjid* and *madrasa*,
Islamic students finger their beads—
neat beards and clean white dress—
As-salaam aleikum and His Mercy and care.
May He lead you always in the bright way of hope.

In sweet Bayyada, the moon
opens in evening a portal of light
above Beit Shahbander's shadowy court.
Masaa al Khair, evening of goodness.
Masaa an Nur, evening of light.
Ahmed brings me cold water
then does his prayers
in the room where Allah touched him once.
Ablution, prostration. Hands cupped around ears,
alert for Mercy.
Jasmine, gardenia, grape vine make my church.

Time for the call to prayers again.
Salat al 'Isha, the prayer of night.
Allahu akbar—God most great.
Subhan-Allahi wa bihamdihi.
I seek God's shelter from Satan, cursed, condemned.
I seek Allah's shelter in leaf and light,
in the Mercy that rises and drifts and saturates all.

Eye Contact in Damascus

My first sunset in Damascus:
the balcony of Room 37
of Fondoq Boorj Alaa
permits a view of half of the horizon.

The sun drops behind a dust-brown tenement.
A woman in white scarf,
appears in an open window
where the sun would be

if the building didn't block it.
She is folding children's clothes,
enjoying the evening air.
I would like for her to know

how her simple and essential work cheers me,
far as I am from home.
Seeing me, she fiercely shutters the window,
closing out the light and air, along with me.

Sunbeams, angling from behind her wall,
silhouette the rooftop antennae, guy-lines, utility boxes,
vent pipes, oil drums, the satellite dishes
tilted as though to anoint the city with their catch of light.

The crown of the Cham Palace Hotel goldens
above a rush of unanointed taxis and pedestrians,
car horns, police whistles, growl of tires and brakes,
the heat and dodge of a busy city. The breeze

nudges the leaves of *The Book of Common Prayer*.
Give peace, O Lord, in all the world.
Aloud, for all of us, I utter the response:
For only in You can we live in safety.

Today I fasted, wandering a world of unfamiliar voice,
afraid to step into the streets,
afraid to buy a meal, reveal myself
an alien.

I think of the woman, ashamed.

4

The barren hilltops wall Damascus
from the world, encircle the city
like a mother's arms.

A loudspeaker crackles the call to prayer.
A satellite dish obscures
the minaret.
I listen.

Words beyond words
lift me with deep and sudden peace.
A man watches me from the building across the street.
From where he is he sees

the horizon I cannot see. We meet
with a wave like worlds traveling in different directions
suddenly finding themselves
in the same orbit.

Calligraphy in Pink

Pink Floyd brings to mind
a shade of brick that should be loved,
the ink she wrote her letters in,
that albino I encountered in
Damascus once.

His skin yes pink not white.
Hair white, his lips.
He was asking (in French) the way
to Saladin's grave, "knight without fear or blame . . ."
The dumb-founded sheikh
was mute.

She spoke in the hue
of her favorite flowers.
>*I love you forever.*
>*Do you remember? Why are you cruel?*
>*Don't leave me ever.*

The sun was brutal that day.
The pink man seemed to sizzle.
The sheikh rubbed his chin
as he turned away.

Pink roses.
Carnation.
Albino skin.

Nearest the Mosque

The nearer the mosque you live, they say,
the more blessed you are.
But Loutfi grumbles every day
about the dawn prayer.

He says the *muezzin* might as well
be standing in his ear.
He rakes the fire and sets the kettle
on for tea. "Look here,

never mind," says Abu Bakr,
the *muezzin*, with a laugh.
"You won't rise to do *Salaat al Fajr*
forever.
          Soon enough

you'll have all day
to sleep, and night as well, and not
wake up at all to pray."
From the smoke, Loutfi lifts the pot

and pours, faking a yawn.
He knows what the *muezzin* knows.
That's why before each dawn,
just when the sweet voice calls, he throws

his bedding off and wakes
to splash ice water on his feet
and face, then stepping lightly makes
his way across the street.

IWAN: ENTERING

The Ripe and the Unripe Fruit

The unripe can't understand what it feels like
to be ready.

Jalaluddin Rumi

In the season of melon and cantaloupe,
The grapes cannot know their own luscious ripeness,
The heavy readiness to let go of the vine.

The green wheat just beginning to sprout,
Like some poor child, all vanity and ego,
Thinks it wants to be young forever.

When pistachios crackle open
By moonlight, they are joyfully sighing,
Why did we not know?

Control: Hiking in Arkansas and Syria

1.

I once led a hike to the top of Rich Mountain.
After ten tiring miles,

we stopped at the widow's place to rest and eat.
We swam in the cool river.

Later, relaxed and full,
I took the wrong fork.

We wandered in a swamp a swamp for an hour.
No one was aware.

The others trusted I knew the path, treacherous
and thick with briers,

spiders, mud, and moccasins—no path at all.
No one knew my terror.

They followed, singing songs, exclaiming
at the dark beauty

of that way. At last we cleared the swamp,
its rotting smell,

and came upon the road I knew, winding
ahead to the foot

of the familiar mountain. No one knew my relief,
my joy. No one shared

my heart's feast
of finding the way.

2.

I am free to let go here, be led
by others, who know the way.
I do not have to calculate the distance

or choose the crossing.
No point. Impossible. I have no map
of this country in my head.
The others know the peaks and passes,
and I follow them over the hills
and into night as a child heels
to his mother. This trust
is liberating. With the shepherd
leading, I graze on scenery
without thinking. I delight in the wild
wheat scattered for travelers.
When the way becomes rocky and steep
I can center all my energy and breath,
aid my muscles with grateful prayers.
Letting go of will, of the need
to lead and control, leaves me
where I can find my way without falling.
Letting go lets me be aware of something
more than my destination:
each small step,
here and now,
the moment passing.

Suleiman Street Station

From Golgotha the buses come and go.
The skull stares down on those who board
for Bethlehem, Hebron, and Jericho.
Exhaust and clamor drift toward

the garden tomb where God was laid to rest,
garden fresh with blossom, leaf, and vine,
shady paths, stone paths, olive press,
the largest found in Palestine.

In the field where thieves were crucified, we stare
at watches, sweat and wait, keen to keep
appointments. What makes that cliff appear
to scowl? What makes his old eyes weep?

Excursion in Syrian Mesopotamia

Because my mother's name
is Zenobia
I am admitted free to the ruins
of Mari
as if a descendant of the sand

A maze of mud brick walls
collapsed charred
courtyard and palace
secret passages under a canvas roof
raised by the Archaeological Society

The guide tells the story
of lost tourists
discovered raving
after three missing days
a tale of ghosts and skeletons

And here I sit at my keyboard
changed to a lunatic
frothing with anger
having discovered my origin
in ancient violence

The Donkeys of Al Jalla

The *ajnabi* is impressed by dignity
under heavy loads, sacks stuffed with fodder, wheat,
weigh on their backs with boys
who slap their flanks with sticks.

Sunrise at *Salhiye* we bargained
with the watchman on the price of a ticket, and lost.
Now we have come from Mesopotamian Mari.
Two French tourists disappeared there once,

found three days later shrieking of bones
and howling skulls. The locals have seen their desert
dancing. Whoever joins them goes insane.
One sees the donkeys limping through streets,

past the *suq* where cold Mandarin is sold,
past huts with painted slogans: "ONE ARAB NATION."
Jihad, who drives the *service*, says,
"Those relics probably had slogans, too."

A donkey limps in the road and stops.
We stop. Jihad plays the horn with relish.
Malek, whose village this is, says, "It seems
we abuse our donkeys here."

Here villagers abused fifty French troops
and dumped their corpses into Al Fraa,
across which, later, we row, tasting the water
as if in it might linger the flavor of Eden.

Women in bright clothes are pulling wheat,
the donkeys browse on stubble.
In the room where we slept Malek showed a chart
of the prophets. Jesus, who chose a donkey's colt,

had thirty-three years, the Prophet (peace be upon him)
sixty-three when he died. The villagers lay
in cotton fields to shoot. The baffled French,
of many ages, died.

The village chief was a man, but stubborn. Arrested, hanged.
One cannot say with what dignity he dangled, but
the French no longer rule the land,
and the clear Euphrates flows on.

I will nap on the Pullman, wake somewhere near Raqqa
to see a brown village, huts and tents,
and on a hill a Muslim cemetery, stony, dry,
with a solitary donkey grazing.

The Cedars

The cedars of Lebanon
for sale on the Internet.
WORLDWIDE DELIVERY IN 72 HOURS

Why would you buy a cedar?

Token of long life:
bless the birth of a son.
Token of eternal love:
bless the wedding, bless the marriage.
Grow something holy.

The symbol of Lebanon depicted
in outstretched hands,
a tender sprig in a palmful of dirt.
I imagine the seedling's roots
contending with Texas caliche
like faith against the skull
of a greedy man.

Up from Bsharre
above the valley of Beqaa
the crowded *service* chased itself
around hairpin turns.
We stopped to smoke, buy melons, and piss.
A man was sick in the ditch.
We climbed into Solomon's dreams.
The shops were selling cedar crosses.

On a hill near the grove
Christ and the thieves sway above the crowd
carved in the old growth, crucified
in the bare, dead branches.

The wood of these trees
has built palaces, temples, homes, fleets,
the engines of war.
From Babylon, from Assyria, from Egypt, from Rome,
many have climbed the cloudy slopes
to cut the heartwood.

18

Nebuchadnezzar boasted: "On Mount Lebanon
I cut down mighty cedars
with my pure hands."

The Lord of Jinn and men,
by whose power
Nebuchadnezzar grazed on grass,
raised your hills,
O Lebanon,
pushed the crust of the earth,
crushed plates together
in a mighty crash.
Jerusalem remembers
the logs that fell from your snowy peaks.

Save a species facing extinction!
Plant your own cedar!

Wherever there is piety,
wherever there is hunger and thirst for righteousness,
wherever there is kingly greed and vanity,
wherever there is delight of the eyes and desire for power,
the foundations of the world
will forever receive your rare beams, O Lebanon.

Order Now

The Beginning of the Desert

They said it was the beginning of the desert,
unbroken brown—only scattered clumps
of stiff grass and a little air to breathe to show
it wasn't the moon. How could it feed the flocks?
The women stayed near the hand-woven tents.
The sociable shepherds in black cloaks
with faces a thousand years old, three thousand,
years uncountable as the stones, a wealth
of stones between each knot of gray vegetation.

They said it was the beginning of the desert,
wind blowing chill, snow on distant peaks
as we wound east toward Lebanon.
We reached the bath above Abu Rabbah.
A woman, a man, and a child in the steam.
She knelt with her face in his lap,
as though resting or worshiping.
The boy sat by, apparently bored. One son
was not enough, so in the vapor they bathe
for the sake of fertility.

The ruins of the old bath just below,
yellow arches and fallen stones and shadows.
And above, on the edge of the world, a castle,
a windbreak for lighting cigarettes.
They called it *Badiya*, the place you see forever.
The brown plain below us naked at sunset.
Where does life come from if not underground,
if not dropped from stars over the empty land,
if not kicked from the stones as we pass?

Stalk

I have not died enough. Not yet.
This shoot
of sensuality keeps sprouting
from the stump.
I would be wind, all air, invisible path to the dark, stable center.
But the knot-headed wood
returns, insisting, born
to creep on slight, pallid tracks of light.

Ramallah

The bus departs below the skull.
A young man starts a conversation
in my language. *Where do you go?*
I also. You are very welcome.

His age my son's. What he studies,
and what I teach. An hour of this.
The bus pours us out in a dirty *suq*.
Now we walk. The wall I came

to see snakes through hills, diminishing
with distance as if in shame.
He helps me through the checkpoint. Soldiers
with computers, guns know they can never

be safe. A man is sitting on
the ground, his hands are cuffed behind him.
His eyes refuse to know me.
                                           This
is my dead father.

The student looks at me: *Sir, what*
did you just say? He takes my arm,
he leads me to the city center,
begs me stay with him, come to

his house, let him guide me wherever
I want to go. He knows that I
will soon be lost. He does not know
I must be lost, must walk where I

am different, walk through every
quarter, walk out of my habits until
the jostling crowd rubs off my skin,
rubs off illusions, until the noise

of the alleys, lanes, and streets muffles
the confidence of cherished myth,
drowns the whispers of religion,
until the sun cooks me and I

become the one not lost, having
come to my home in dispossession.
One day I will bring my son here,
show him where and how I died.

SAHN: GATHERING AND ABLUTION

Nasruddin

the fool

calls me

home with

a joke

Border Crossing

When you go in search of what you want
the world to be, expect a long journey.
Expect deserts, battlefields, ghettoes,
ghost towns, hurricanes, bullets.

Expect lost luggage and ruined houses, walls
to climb or go around.
The bus you ride on will be cramped,
hot, sweaty, smelling of animals.

You will walk a lot, under moonlight
and sunlight, stones bruising your feet.
You will have trouble with schedules.
Your connecting flight will leave

too early, too late, without you,
cancelled or delayed.
Too much time at stations, waiting,
or not enough.

When you cross borders you will unpack everything,
show your whole life to the yawning guard,
repack with haste to keep the line moving.
It will almost always be night

when you arrive in a strange country
in search of what you want
the world to be.
When you walk from the station at dawn

into a city of strange words,
walk as if you are home, ready to live now
in the dancing that you see,
in the world as it actually is.

Man with No Legs

Young man, you scooting along Shari' al Quatli at twilight on
    legless hams
You with your filthy trousers and hands
You with your face in the crotches and asses of every passerby
You with your supplications invoking before Allah your right to
    charity
You with your expression nevertheless matter-of-fact and
    unexpectant
You whom we struggle not to see
Are you my brother?

You don't know my language nor I yours
And this is but the beginning of what we do not know

They buy bread in the markets
They peer through the windows of Al Barra to study the prices on
    new refrigerators
They pause in the shops for flowers and candy
They take their chances in front of taxis and tour busses
They glance in the travel agencies at posters of destinations to
    which they will never journey
They smash cigarette butts with their shoes, take a few steps, and
    light another
They say *as-salaam* and good evening, forming wishes remote as a
    moon rising through dust
They are the true amputees, dismembered as they are from one
    another
And I am one of them.

Who blames the Cosmos for its anger?
Who blames them for their rage at the Cosmos?
Not you, my brother, surely.
Not one so humble as to sweep the street with your buttocks
Not one so humble as to take upon yourself the grime of the city
You must have learned from the refuse a wisdom beyond us
The pavement has spoken to you with the weight of all those
    footsteps
You have claimed from the gutter what others rejected
You have polished your existence with the grit of what's trampled

You will forgive me for seeing only your body

Forgive my pity for your missing parts
Forgive my envy for the power of your misshapen thighs
Forgive my disgust for your stench and filth
Forgive my nonchalance and self-congratulation
Forgive my fear and horror
Forgive my denial, O least of these, whom to deny is rejection and
 death
Forgive me, O God.

And what can I do for penance, my brother,
But dig in my pockets for a few lira and pass on into the night
My love and humanity
Calloused as your stumps
By the grit and stones of the streets?

Camping on Mt. Sinai

In the true and inhuman night of Sinai
where the nearest village is miles away
we speculate to kill the time on constellations
we know little about.
We find the Dipper (Wagon, German Sophie calls it),
polestar,
Orion's belt and curving Draco, horses, hunters, bears
and dragons, clear as legends on a map
of territories which never existed.

Just yesterday we met on the bus.
This morning we visited the Charnel House
and then bought groceries.
The bones of monks in brown heaps.
Their empty eyes watchful sockets.
Old Stephen the Porter kept his seat
(the guidebook says)
before penitents passing to the Path of Moses,
along which (later) we fed orange peels to dromedaries
(stepping so as to avoid their droppings).
Their Beduin drovers bummed cigarettes,
hawked rides to tourists to near the top
for a few pounds only.
The Law was given on stone,
a heavy, hard, and brittle substance, cold.
The Chapel of the Burning Bush
was closed.

Each day the so-called pilgrims come
to watch the sunset or sunrise
from the peak of Gabal al-Mousa.
We camp up there to see them both
and to save money. The desert night turns cold.
We shiver, waiting, beneath rented blankets,
spread in the ruins of an ancient chapel,
and can say this about the sky
beneath which our ancestors wandered:
these conjured shapes spin on.

The moon rises finally, obscuring

31

our constellations, lighting the steps
from Elijah's Basin to the Cave of Moses
as if the mountain itself were glowing.

A Civil War

Sleepless in the dark, in the apartment of the dentist,
my host in Beirut,
I hear the bombs exploding in Tripoli.

Israel is destroying the power plant again.
The wall of this building is pocked with bullets
from the civil war.

There is nothing civil about war,
says the dentist's neighbor.

She is Serbian, a prostitute.
She has her window open.
She is hearing the bombs falling, too.

A Small Boat on the Euphrates

One dervish to another: "What was your vision of God's presence?"
Jalaluddin Rumi, "The Question"

For a hundred lira (too much, Malek says)
a boy named Karim works the oars
against wind and current, water clear and cold
here where the bodies of French soldiers drifted
after the massacre near Al Jalla. Imagine blood,
the determined stares, relaxed arms waving
to the blue bottom,
surprising the fish and frogs of Al Fraa.

The Turks and Syrians contend for this stream.
They say it flows from Paradise.
The boat swings out toward the center, steered
with an easy skill. I snap pictures, corpses bump the stern.

Along the shores, families harvest wheat.
I dip a hand and taste the life of the river.
Karim pauses, stares.
One who drinks, Malek says, will always return.
His grandfather was among those who ambushed the French,
who later dragged them to the edge
and dumped them in.

Vision of Miriam

According to my president this country sponsors terror.
This claim discourages the tourists,
but Mary likes to visit anyway.

The politicians have forgotten Mashta al Helou,
with its cool summers, Mediterranean air,
so the people have it pretty good here,
going about their business of boiling corn.

From here you can visit ruined castles.
Safita, Salahiddin, the Krak des Chevaliers
visible beyond the peaks and valleys.

From heaven you can view the whole world's suffering.
From heaven pain is pain.
No matter who or where or what the cause.
When you enter that kingdom
put away your passport.
Nobody demands a form that states
your "State of Origin."
There "ethnic cleansing" means to cleanse
of ethnic hate.
The shade of skin's no more
germane than the color of fur
to a lover of cats.

So Mary comes to this pinnacle
they call the Mountain of the Lady.
She's not particular who sees her here.
The good and not so good
can catch a glimpse.
Muslim, Christian. Religious, not religious.
Children, women, men. Anyone
with eyes to see the human shape of love.

These folk have built a simple shrine.
Of course they paint it blue.
They trek here once a year
up the narrow, steep, and twisting road from the town square.

Something they can do together.

A Eucharist at the Canary Hotel

We meet in the garden at the Fondoq Canary.
The evening cool is coming, each of us
alone with quiet little thoughts of night,
fatigue from travel, day's business done.
As-salaam and the cheerful tea.
I invite him to my table, fellow wanderer.

Here in a time of war, he asks my homeland.
I am from America, from the State of Texas.
(Is my voice apologetic?)
With a grin, more mischievous than malicious,
he says, *Like Bush. My name is Hamad, I am Iraqi, from Tikrit,
the home Saddam.* He could be a double,
same age, same eyes, same moustache,
strong, proud features and body.

He is in Jordan two weeks, on business,
he says, a furniture merchant, he says.
Perhaps believing I would doubt his word,
he shows me four identity cards,
his passport and business card.
For all he knows I might be CIA.
For all I know he might be recruiting insurgents.
He does not hide his anger.
He says Halab, where I say I am going, is beautiful.
Tikrit, he says, was beautiful, too.
When I say I would like to visit, he says,
It is danger. I say I hear it is bad there now.

Yes, very bad, he says, and to show me how
he says the mother of his wife
bought a fish from the River of Tikrit
and in its belly found
a human finger.
He tells me this beneath jasmine and moonlight,
tells me this and more.

Under Saddam he had it good, he says.
Electricity, water, food. His four children
went to university for free.

His daughter majored in English.
The good life ended when Americans came.

In Baghdad, where he lives these days, he says,
the soldiers entered his house three times,
their guns aimed at his children,
rifle at his throat.
They said it was their job.
From his passport, he says, they stole $50.
It not belonging to Saddam, he shouts. *My money! I work!*
He clinches, sweats, remembering his fear,
his impotency and rage, his stolen dignity.

The waiter brings fresh tea.
I ask for *hummos* and bread,
offer Hamad one of my smokes.
American? he asks. I think he might refuse,
but takes it with a nod, wishing me health as I light it.
With a deep exhale of smoke, he says,
This war between governments, not people,
but people die—Americans, Iraqis.

His country is full of foreigners causing death—
Iranians, Saudis, Jordanians, Syrians.
His river is full of fish full
of the pieces of children
killed by American bombs.
And for what? For oil, for Israel,
for the liar Bush.
But Bush will not win,
Cheney, Rumsfeld will not win.
I win. The merchants win.
The war is good for business.
Everybody needs furniture.

The jasmine throw their silent fragrance
on the shadows. Our sugary tea grows cold.
The waiter brings the *hummos* and bread.

I tear a loaf,
offer him bread,
hope aloud for peace and better days.

We will kiss on the cheeks when he leaves.
For now he eats and says, *I used to love the fish.*
I never can eat that dish again.

To Those Who Would Kill Me
Because I'm American

I want to think of you
bathing your baby.
Your sleeves are rolled.
Water mats the hair of your arms.
You soap her skin with a soft cloth,
the scent of bay leaves.
Water and soap, a true ablution.
Your voice comes out.
There is no *fatwa* in your talk.
Your daughter laughs, splashes your beard.
The hands that hold your weapons
lather her fine hair.
She reaches for your face, her eyes
find yours forever.

I too would like to stop
whatever threatens her.
We have that much
in common.

Crossing

Long I dreamed of crossing the Jordan,
observing the country where so many mad
and sorrowful prophets fished
and bathed. Would the banks
be stained, the water black or red from so much sin?
Would the air howl with a heavenly hellish light?

My time came, I was crossing the Jordan.
But on the bus that carried me
across the King Hussein Bridge,
a man from Amman began to speak
of his sister in Ohio, sick with M.S.,
tortured in health, calling him to say:

What will I do? What will I do?
No one will want me.

I listened, and forgot the Jordan,
the scene out the window of the bus.
I forgot the sad and angry prophets,
repentance and grace. I shut
my eyes, imagining life and love
for the one no one will want.

Long Walk

When you walk all day with someone
and neither knows the other's language,
you will find much to talk about.

Rafik is Arab. His letters are sun and moon.

On the *maseer*, the "long walk," where we meet,
we pass through orange groves, olive groves,
through the ancient rugged country, up

and down a twisting way.

Taking my arm, he says a hundred times, "Hello."
His only word of English. "Hello"—again and again
until it becomes HOL-low, hilloh, HAY-L-O-O-O-O—

just to break the silence with a bright, round nimbus of speech.

He gives me cigarettes, food, plucks
oranges from the trees to sweeten my walk.
When we come to a village, I am

the first to drink the cold well water. When dark comes

to "Hyena Heaven," and I am
so tired, he points his torch
before my feet

to light the treacherous path.

Without light, without food or smokes,
how can I reciprocate?
"*Shukran*." Thanks.

That is my one word.

Well, that was years ago.
Rafik has learned a little English,
I a little Arabic.

Meeting half way like this,

41

we find
more and more to say,
more and more in the wordless quiet

our footsteps leave.

MINBAR

Bimaristan Arghun

> Return now to the street which led south to the Bab
> Kinnesrin. 100 m. on the left is the Maristan Arghun al-
> Kamili converted from a house to an asylum in 1354 by the
> Mameluke Governor, Arghun al-Kamili. The entry is
> through a tall, honey-combed portal leading through a
> vestibule to the central courtyard. Diagonally across is a
> tall vaulted passage leading to a confined octagonal court-
> yard designed to house the dangerously insane. A central
> fountain is surrounded by twelve cells, still used to house
> chained inmates at the beginning of this century.
> Ross Burns, *Monuments of Syria*

The wealth and benevolence of Arghun al Kamili
provided here for the dangerous insane
an asylum of darkness, water, bread, and stone.
The walls have absorbed their wails, their stench,
their outrageous laughter in a honeycomb of cells
like the chambered heart of Aleppo.

This organ leaks into the lanes and *suqs*,
arteries of color and life unchanged since Arghun.
The devout still pour into mosques to pray,
and merchants bargain over blood-red rugs
and polished gold, brighter than sunbeams carved
in the sandstone arches in the "house of patients."
An old man reclines near the door of a shadowy *khan*,
greets the stranger with an ancient peace. Children sew
in the sweat shops, or quarrel over soccer in the alleys,
munch white grapes and pears at the stalls
near Bab Qinnasrin with its four doors,
its four desperate defenses.
Women kindle fires to cook the evening meal
in the very bastions from which
defenders of the city once poured boiling oil
and shot their arrows into the hearts
of other women's men. The smells of food
and human waste, all manner of rubbish, blown
against old stones scored by the chisels
of Hittite or Mameluke. Under the full moon
the first rain of October has broken summer's drought,
refreshed the night air, and turned the lanes to mud.

A boy carries a baby with a dirty face.
A vendor clangs the lid on his pot of boiled corn.
From balconies hang ivy and grape, the metal doors
of the houses, heavy and austere
as the great iron ball which defended Bab al Antakya.

The tourists hail taxis outside the Great Mosque.
A minaret of the Citadel ascends
preposterously in the distance above
the modern pandemonium of the oldest city on earth,
my Aleppo,
which gleams and gushes in its busy, vital procession.
As the shops close, the old town goes to its nightly rest
as frantic in its ease as the pulse
of a soldier resting after indecisive struggle,
savoring coffee and *arghieleh*, though uncertain if
tomorrow's assault will *in shaa' llah* bring victory
or death or more of the same.

That loving soul Arghun al Kamili was wise among men.
Where life is thickest and most sweet,
we cannot be far from madness.

One Morning I Find a Bone

One early morn I find up on my terrace
A bone. How it got there is mysterious.
In the woods I would have thought a sly hyena,
Audacious and night-prowling, dragged it there as
A sign of cunning. But four flights up, no stairs?
No, impossible to reach. And not even a
Nolan Ryan in his prime could have chunked
So high this lightweight splintered fragment.
From a large animal, human for all I know, cleft
A few inches below a knobby joint, the shaft
Well-chewed, sucked clean of marrow,
Its shattered end a deformed mouth, which spoke
For God a grotesque warning not to smoke,
Take vitamins and milk for skeletal health,
Heaven is the only place to lay up wealth.
No Yorick's skull, but I ache even so
To contemplate this dry memento
Of some savage cleaving, leaving for all
With ears to hear an old and obvious moral:
The Law of the Jungle—eat and be eaten
And have what's left on some sun-beaten
Rooftop dropped by a crow. (How else?
It surely didn't walk here by itself.)
O dread design of night,
That brought to stony height
Bone-bearing bird in kindred flight,
Et cetera, et cetera, et cetera. How bleak
Dodge that thought and meditate
On phallic bone in phallic beak,
That bleached and eloquent almanac
Of procreative energy and light,
Of raw rebirth and bodily ascension,
Of bare-boned faith, against the gravity of reason,
In the power that will gather in a certain season
A thousand shards of clay scattered off in
A thousand directions, each *memento mori*
For some drowsy hermit lying in his coffin
To call to mind with a shiver before he
Achieves (who knows how long?) oblivion.

47

Religion in Syria

Emberha—yesterday—one day nearer the end
of days than the day before—
in *'Adeliya* Mosque, the Sufis swayed
and sang the name of God a thousand times.
Ali, in beatnik beard and dress,
arrived a quarter hour late,
such freedom celebrated here
in hearts that love the Lord of Jinn and men.

Sahaat Farhat, the square of churches.
A sweating tourist enters the gate
of the Marionite Church in weary thirst.
A man filling bottles at a drinking fountain
gives cold water to the foreigner.

During dinner at *Beit Wakil*,
we hear the *muezzin*'s call to pray, faint and lovely,
from *Jaami' Kabir*. Our friend
excuses herself and asks the *maitre d'*
for the nearest mosque or quiet place.
In America, she's less embarrassed than here
to tell the people she wants to pray.
"Americans are more spiritual," she says,
respectful of her conscience and faith.
Walid discourses on the heart's instinctive search for truth.
He cites those martyred heretics who say
Love is the true and only creed:
Love Jehovah, Allah, God; love all created things.
Bass. Khalas. It's enough.
Though stuffed with *khubz* and *aperitif,*
we cut and share the last of the meat
so the lamb will not have died in vain.

Edenic Bayyada, soft and shady this Friday morn.
From neighboring mosques,
I hear *Al Juma'* sermons loud with rage.
The preacher raves
against bad Muslims who neglect Qur'an and prayers,
love not the Prophet,
cheat and steal, and let their lands be overrun.

The threats of death and fire appall.

The Sufi *sheikh*, among his books
stuffed with *fatwa* and *sunna* commentary
served ice cold non-alcoholic beer
in bright green bottles as if to prove
the Way does not hinder or deprive what's good.

Those who've found a way to love
want those they love to find that way.

We savor *rutab* from Persian Iran.
The Lord in his mercy gave such dates
to frightened and laboring Miriam, mother of Christ,
succor from the pangs of birth.
Sweet and soft as jelly,
they might have been packaged in Paradise.
Serve with *ahwe* and conversation.

A student of mine, and friend,
worked in Saudi Arabia a year
for the purpose of making money and *Hajj*.
He won't go back. Better, he says, to serve two years
in Syria's army than be a slave to the sons of the rich.
His luggage went missing on his pilgrimage.
Clothes, camera, mobile, all he owned
he left and went to stone the devil,
but the devil went and stole his bags.
Forced to make his way to friends in only a towel.
Glory to God who commands all things.

Dar al Islam, some will say, includes all
who believe in the oneness of God.
But others insist *sunna* and *shari'a* are needed to save.
Believe in the Prophet and his ways
or fiery hell waits.
The Muslim who converts to Christ
can have no church or Eucharist.
The priest just after baptizing him
told Mahmoud to never return.
He studies alone a smuggled Bible,
lonely communion of water and bread,
estranged from the churches of the Christian Quarter,

the crowded cathedrals of *Azizieh*
where the blue-clad Virgin stands in every window and nook.
Kineesa Latin, Orthodox, Protestant, Syriac, Greek.

> *"No compulsion in religion."*
> *"We could have made you one people,*
> *but we made you to vie in righteous deeds."*

Jaami' Tawhid, the Unity Mosque, stands in the midst
of many churches, proudly proclaiming God the One
to all who worship the Lord in Three.
Creed is a box to hold the Lord.
Hadith says
if all the oceans were filled with ink,
it would not be enough
to write what could be written of Him.

A lone sheep bleats in the back of a truck.
Black face and dirty white fleece,
red spot sprayed on its rump
to mark this lamb for slaughter and feast.
Halal. We slit its throat
with the name of God, we cut
the vein to drain the blood.
(*"We are close to you*
as your jugular vein!")
The streets at *'Eid*
turn to streams of animal blood.
Hides and fleeces dry in the burning sun
while *khubz* bloats on the hot *tannur.*
Ramadan ending, fast complete,
we gather our families, chat and eat.

Halal is the lamb.
Haram is the pig.
Halal is laughter, dates, kabob, *inshaallah.*
Haram is the bare-tanned arms of women.
Halal is the cooling evening wind.
Haram is the wine, the *arak*, luck, for all things happen by the will
of God.
Haram those evil ones made of fire.
Haram the hypocrite, infidel.

50

Halal is *zeit* poured over *leban*.
Halal are the spices, cheeses, faithful friend.

We feed the pigeons at *Housh al Bayyada*
dry white corn flat as lentil.
Ahmed, agricultural engineer, asked a farmer friend for some.
Now three man-sized hundred kilo bags
are stacked beneath the stairs,
enough to feed our birds a hundred years.
They watch for cats and peck at corn;
our tea steeps under shady vines—
uzkuru allah, the pigeons say.
Ya'ni, Razan explains, an imperative:
uzkuru allah.

    "Say
    the name
    of God"

the pigeons say,
calling from trellis, drain spout, window.
When worried or lonely, make *Du'a*,
calling on God, conversing with God, and asking His will.

We spread white corn by the Lord's great will.
It sprouts and grows in the cracks
below the grapevine and umbrella plants.

Mercy and trial,
bad and good—
in *Halab*, the city of milk,
we live and love by the Lord's great will.

Pulling Weeds

It's best to do it after rain
when their conspiracy with dirt
is at its weakest. Their hurt
is audible. A muffled scream,
the delicate fibers tearing, as they cling
to their spot of earth.

You might smash a ladybug,
dislodge a pillbug with a vicious tug
or a nut with cloven shell
just sprouting where it fell
into what would be a tree.

Often they grow in a cluster
so that one root undoes another
or one from the others gains strength.
You lose a morning, and your hands
are blackened green by sod.
Your back and hams
ache from bending until you forget God
Himself made these to strive also
for the light. You think, Oh
if only I could make peace
with the weeds. If only they would not hog the whole
green yard but settle for a little piece
and leave the rest autonomous.

As thorough and meticulous
as you try to be,
some of them—the ones who chose
the hardest soil, the ones whose
stems are most fragile—stubbornly break
at the soil line, leaving their
long pointed roots like broken stakes,
driven deep,
to mark their range.
The taller ones have already flowered
and spread their spoors so that though
their bodies may be cast into a pile to be dried
by the sun, mulched or burned,

you know
that like all despised
unwanted things, they will return.

After Dinner at Dr. Zafari's House

They seem familiar, these photographs,
the wounded and dead of Palestine—young men
whose deaths amount to a few paragraphs
in the *Times*, on CBS and CNN.
Now this one stares—his dead eyes shoot regret
and dread—from a blood-stained gurney, while
the doctor and his Arab friends fret
about what must be done, rage and revile.
How will I sleep tonight? The corpses will
come at me like the bullets of history
and I will wince and apologize until
the one lying there on the sheet is me.
What are words like *justice, homeland, free*?
We put away the photos, drink our tea.

Young Palestinian Explodes Bomb; No Injuries Reported

Noor's first cousin himself did explode,
So his father I called to console.
"Don't do that," he said,
"For my son is not dead,
"But in Paradise prances his soul.

"In his house here we celebrate well,
"For his brave deeds are really quite swell.
"Yes, my son is a martyr,
"Not a one there is smarter—
"Though no Zionist sent he to Hell."

Homeland Security Raises Alert Status; FEMA Advises Duct Tape and Plastic

I fall asleep Voltaire, and Kafka I
awake, the joke of chaos duct-taped to
the cage of reason. Armageddon, high
on the President's list of things to do
before the next election, seems to be
as certain as a strip search. To protest a war
is friendship to the tyrant. No one can see
the common enemy. *Allahu akbar!*
Where is your light, Voltaire, O you who jeer
at Jesuits mining gold from genocide
and baste those Moslem Turks who satisfied
their cravings with flank steak carved from the rear
of a living girl? It's as dark as when you died;
the *Ungeziefer* kicks at the black air.

Graves of the Holy Land

The dead lie
in the land.

We say God says
this land is ours.

They say God says
this land is theirs.

They lie, we lie
in the land.

Summit

What if God convened a summit?

What if He said to Israel and Palestine
The silence of tombs is one silence
Because you could not be honest with even your own people
Because the only peace you could imagine was the peace of
    separation
Because you forgot that the land belongs to Who made it
I have no more to do with you forever?

What if He said to America
A dove cannot be an eagle
The beak of your hawk is a spear in the side of your Savior
Because you wanted safety more than justice
I have no more to do with you forever?

What if He said to the Jews
The temple is gone forever
Because you pledged death and used a pretence of faith to multiply
    wailing
I have no more to do with you forever?

What if He said to Hamas and Hezbollah the Irgun and Yishuv
    and ZOA
And to every soldier policeman and freedom fighter
Because you despised a single creature and belittled the work of
    My hands
I have no more to do with you forever?

What if He said to the leaders of the Nations
The impotent should not pretend to power
Because you were timid before history
I have no more to do with you forever?

What if He said to the kings of Arabia
    to all the kings of the West
You have your reward and it will be bitter
Because you loved power and honor
    and shut your ears and slept well
    and gestured and made loud noises
    and sent troops to protect and expand your own borders

I have no more to do with you forever?

What if He said to the grieving mothers of Israel and Palestine and
    the whole world
Because you wept for your child and no other
I have no more to do with you forever?

What if He said to the citizens of America
Because you listened to politicians
    and surrendered your mind to lies
    and refused to think it might matter
Because you demanded freedom and justice for yourselves
    and turned your back on freedom and justice for others
Because you settled for plenty and grew fat in the plenty
    and the plenty was not enough
I have no more to do with you forever?

What if He said to a woman in Texas
Because you were not disturbed
    but rocked and said nothing
    while you held your child in peace
    and your sister's child cried in hunger amid bullets
    and your sister raged and despaired
I have no more to do with you forever?

What if He said to the father whose son died a martyr in his arms
Because you exposed your son to madness
    and cut his throat on the altar of hatred
I have no more to do with you forever?

What if He said to boys throwing stones
Because you threw innocence away with the stones
Because your joy was in blood
I have no more to do with you forever?

What if He said to the mob
Because you loved murder and martyrdom more than life
I have no more to do with you forever?

What if He said to the writer and journalist and speechmaker
Because you threw your words in a whirlwind
I have no more to do with you forever?

What if He said to Christians
Because you worshiped your Prince of Peace with rockets
Because you found your safety in tanks
Because you nailed Love to a cross of indifference
I have no more to do with you forever?

What if He said to Muslims
There is not one spot of ground less holy than another
Because you were not Muslim
I have no more to do with you forever?

What if He said to the Jews
Because you shattered My tablets
    crushed O man both justice and mercy
    forgot the first sin and the homelessness of Cain your father
I have no more to do with you forever?

What if He said to those whom He invited to live in His kingdom
Because you refused to live in My kingdom
I have no more to do with you forever?

What if God convened a Summit
    and called it Earth
And all the Lord's creatures sat in attendance
And His voice descended in love
    from a single star
    and from the hooked moon
    and from the peak of Sinai
    and nobody listened
And rose in sorrow and anger
    from bombed neighborhoods
    and from bloody children
    and from fresh graves
    and nobody listened
And flooded the world with fire
    and nobody
    nobody
    nobody
    listened?

Defection

I feel I am on the verge of defecting
to some country which no one can see.
What is that country to which I defect?
I think it will have no government.

Its people will be the unjustly killed,
only they can make good citizens.
In the supermarkets
you will see the covered women and say

Sister.
You will see the cabbages and praise the meek.
The magazines will go unsold. Newspapers yellow.
It will be treason not to love.

Yet not one neighbor
will kill or be killed for the sake of love
or made to suffer in the name of justice.
No one will harm another in God's name.

The word *jihad* will be unknown.
The word *crusade* will mean expulsion.
In this country which no one can see
no barbed wire will divide us and them.

You will learn the names of your neighbors.

Four Letters on the Absconding of His Dogg

Dalmatian ran away. To self a note:
Call *Times*; buy candles, floss, and cigarettes.
Dear Rabbi Dizzle euthanize, devote
the proceeds to the fund for
                        the shortage of spots.
O Miriam, do you recall our cold,
blue lamentations under dogwood trees?
Suppose the Universe a minute old
is one minute old. Our particles freeze.
Beloved, I can't describe the pain. A wish
devoutly expected bleeds, leaving green
coagulations on the brain. Will's fist
pounds your ass to powder in the rain.
Come home, come home! you've missed, you silly bitch,
the Prophet when he passed (p.b.u.h.).

MIHRAB: QIBLA

Allahu akbar

My body is pierced with hooks
of every size, uncountable.
To each is tied a cord, and the cords

stretch tautly into the mist
that surrounds me, pulling my body
in every direction. I cannot see

what demons hold these cords.
But I know them, I know.
I never owned my own life.

A little god snatches every organ.
Bruises surround those hooks
where they enter and leave my skin.

Think of a beautiful fish quivering on rocks
or rocks with the fine sparkle of Paradise
shoveled over you.

Law and order buries the world like ashes
of a thousand eruptions
in words of devotion and praise.

Nous

Thought is a noose to catch the Mind.
But thought can no more catch the Mind
than a thread around the claw of a lion
can tie the lion.

How many struggle for life
and never escape the physical realm?
How many struggle for life
and never embrace the physical realm?

Ants on a walnut
search for cracks in the shell
without tasting it.
We need termite teeth
to reach the meat, just to carry with all our might
some crumb to our queen.

A man can walk, going nowhere,
and tour the Universe.
Such aerobics are healthy.
Wherever you are in infinity
is both center and circumference.

Today the farmers grow melons
without seeds.
Thankfully
the Gardener of the Cosmos
is not so perverted.
                    Each of His melons
has plenty of seeds, and within each one
infinite potential.

No one river
holds all the rain.
Thought forms Mind
into its own shape.

No single cell, occupying its place
in the corpus of the lion,
though it be the heart,
can comprehend the whole beast.

What does the cell become
when it divides, and divides again?
And again.
And again.
What kind of knife makes that happen?
And when does the cell stop being
itself?
When the lion dies?
Or when it grows grateful
for the tiny miracle
                    of its own cleaving?

Prayer Rug

Men whose knees often touch the earth
should become humble enough for heavy loads.

Like a camel their skin becomes hard, a knot
grows on the joint that joins them every day to dust.

Bowing, each whispers secrets to the ground
out of his own heart hard or soft:

God is most great. Defeat my enemy.
Forgive me Lord and lift me up.

One lifts his face to heaven addressing God:
Who is born for this?

Many refuse the dignity of prostration.
And many, even of those who bow, never see

(perhaps because I come between them
and the taste of the grave)

the grace of being bound,
the good of a face brought low to the world.

Qala'at Mohalabeh

The tourist very seldom visits this castle,
remote in the rugged Alawi hills.
Chamomile grows on the mountain.
Shepherds bring flocks to its feet.

Love, the enemy of bastion and tower,
has ruined the fortification.
Love, destroyer of walls,
builds villages of vine-topped houses.

Love offers melon and tea.
Love befriends the foreigner.
Love welcomes to its table
the stranger with different speech.

Love crumbles barracks and glacis,
fills dungeon with vegetation.
What warriors built in strength and hate
cannot survive this climate.

East

I do not know if loving you
is my weakness or my strength,
if I have lost
or found myself,
if I have broken or healed you.
I know that thirst cannot be satisfied in the body
yet the body demands satisfaction.
What might be exists somewhere.
One night stolen from sleep.
One true and solid thing salvaged from dreams.
Time enough for sleep,
there will be time enough.
Time for remembering the tears,
the softness of one night,
the long warmth and tangle of limbs.
Time for the ache that must come.
Time for discovering the beginning.
Time for exploring and explaining,
for poems that say nothing,
for the shy bath,
for the shadow on the terrace and the morning sun.
Time for dissolving logic,
for stirring resolution in black coffee.
The moon fades in the blue morning.
What we've won
surpasses what we've lost.
The sun must set in the west
to rise again in the east.
One life is never enough.
A thousand bodies are not enough.

Jabl al Qalb

for Sheikh Mahmoud Hosseini

I see we both are tunneling deep
in a mountain, digging from opposite sides.
Through stone and darkness
each of us makes a little passage
for wind and light.
At first we are far apart.
It seems we are striving, opposed.
But little by little we are growing close.
Infinity follows us in
as we chip away at the rock
using our same tools of mercy and love.
One day we are bound to meet
in the center,
and light will flow
through the depths of the mountain.

Resting in the Arbor

As simple as salvation,
wind and sun
the sweet green grapes caress.
The bright leaves live to bless,
forbid no one the shade
they give. Should I,
then, also cherished by
the sun and made
of him to ripen only once, deny
my leaf to any passerby?

Without Guide

There was at Palmyra stone upon stone
and stone fallen from stone. A cat
was sleeping in the bath of a queen
beside the monumental lane
where heroes passed in glory, once. I passed
glancing at the signs and wondering.
Beforehand were those two hours
at the terminal in Homs. We sat
in smoke, unable to commune
in speech, but one in our desire to kill
the night until the next bus came.
No agent worth his name would have
allowed his paying *ajnabi*
so long to wait, so I'd have lost
the very moment worth the price
if I had hired my way. I'd have
awaked with other tourists in
some tired hotel to a varicolored
morning meal of bread, tomatoes,
cucumbers, eggs, instead of on
the bumpy bus an hour before dawn,
let out in night and nowhere in
a town too sleepy to notice me.
I'd not have hiked to ruins in
the windy desert cold and crouched,
beside a tomb in blackness with
hands gloved, dogs barking over there
as though at ghosts until first light,
when sunbeams struck the ancient arch
and world appeared again. That day
while tour groups paid in lira at
the Temple of Bel, listening
in Japanese, Italian, French,
and Arabic to proud laments
about the fair Zenobia,
a shepherd waved me off the way
and sat me on his cloak; and all
before us of that ancient town
and all its glory nothing more
than grazing for his flock.
I travel with no guide. I might

miss much, but otherwise I'd miss
what the guide missed. And that would be
everything.

First Maseer

When, after rough climbing, we came into
that orchard, delight ripened on the face
of every hiker: Rafik, Samir, Abu,
Nadia, Nelly, Nur, Khamis, Ghias,
Toukhig, Maggie, Berj, even ageless
Father George. The farmers gave us oranges,

refreshed us on the sunny grass.
Our weariness became pleasure. Rest
intensified the sweetness of the fruit
and of the kind neighbors. Absolute
relief enlarged, almost to decadence,
the ecstasy of exhausted sense.

When, after rough climbing, we come into
that orchard, light bathes us, blessing all,
every body, and we see the true
economy of that old
and wearying way up, how the pain
of every joint prepares us for the gain
of that green field.

The Door

In search of a door,
I entered the house of a dervish.
The dervish welcomed me.
Seated me upon his couch,
Lavished me with candied citron,
    nuts in sweet yogurt,
    grapes and oranges.
Such was my pleasure
I forgot to ask for passage.
I remember nothing of what the dervish said
up to the moment I was leaving.
Then he spoke:
You have passed through the door
through which no man can pass by asking.

IWAN: LEAVING

Horizon

every horizon appears close now
no tree can
                    taste its own fruit

Meat Market in Aleppo

The faces of sheep
grimace from a tub
of their own offal.

*O lamb who takes
the sins of the world.*

Smooth purple fists of flesh
dangle from ropes
of fat and tendon.

Liver, heart, kidneys.
A tray of yellow brains.

Itfadel!
I am welcome
to ground meat sold by kilo.

The bones, stripped
of every fleck of meat,
seem the long-tailed skeletons of children.

In other stalls,
the pale, wet chickens glisten,
displayed with legs

immodestly spread,
naked
among the covered women.

Coordinated Universal Time

Travel reveals the arbitrariness of time.
Longitudes so many hours lost or gained.

Eight a.m. in Petra—sun leaping onto tombs
carved two millennia before,

already hot on my bare neck—is midnight
at my Texas home. The horse

that departs from Enchanted Rock in the dusk
of Alexander's day passes through

the steep-walled Siq drawing a carriage
full of tourists to the bullet-riddled Treasury.

The doors have filled with erosion
from the sandstone cliffs. We measure centuries

in meters of dust,
in civilizations that rose and fell:

Nabatean, Roman, Byzantine, Crusader.
Blood and water drain to level ground

of sand and scrub. An obelisk stands watch
above the valley of ageless Jinn, al-Uzza

and Dushara silent, as the horse sets out again.
From the High Place of Sacrifice, the victims laugh

at those who speak of jet lag, itineraries and count
the hours it takes to reach

by bus Amman or Aqaba, where the tides
forever stir the sea life and the sand.

Abraham Dreams Aleppo

Up here on my terrace I hear what I please
crow wings or the voice of God or the moon
rising over the Mosque of Mercy   yes I hear it
I eat succulent red grapes   crack pistachios with my teeth
I smoke *arghieleh* and follow my thoughts
as if they might have direction significance

Up here on my terrace I count steeples and minarets
and the tops of the cypress aspiring to the same light
I cannot count the satellite dishes
all tilted west on the stained rooftops
numerous as the sons of Ibrahim
sleeping in the cracked stone houses

Up here on my terrace I observe what I please
I pray for enlightenment or lunacy   for anything
besides smothering windless indifference
I make mental notes to tell no one
A man in soiled clothes pushes a cart on the street
collecting garbage

O Father Ibrahim   when you stopped
on that little hill shrouded in dust
what did you hear
besides the feeding and rutting of your livestock
Did you sleep in your tent that night
with visions of citadel and sieges

Did you toss and dream of the steamy *hammam*
of pavement squeezing the roots of locust trees
of busses belching aliens to bargain
for gold and carpets in the covered *suq*
Did you hear the babble of radios
Did you wake and regret leaving your home

Up here on my terrace I tell no lies
I watch the woman in the building across my garden
closing her shutters to undress and the little boy
fetching a clean shirt from the line on his balcony
I stretch and sip tea and wonder
did I do well and is this real

82

Slogan for a Dry Wind

*Does every man of them desire
that he should be made to enter
the garden of bliss? (Al Ma'arij 38)*

Along the lane to Bab al Hadid
the wall on the way to my house
in fresh red paint screams
DEATH TO AMERICA

Housh Shahbander—green vines and flowers
I sit in shade in evening
pondering   DEATH TO AMERICA.
What does this slogan mean?
America, what do *you* mean?

I pass through Bayyada
greetings from children on balconies.
Ahlan from neighbors.
As-salaam from merchants sitting in shops.
Grizzled old men the sheikhs of Bayyada
teach me the Arabic names
for onion, eggplant, watermelon, garlic:
basal banjaan jabbas thum.
Amused by my clumsy accent, but pleased,
they laugh and send me on with a blessing,
return to their tea *'argheile* politics
return to watching the world from their corner.
DEATH TO AMERICA   What does it mean?

The blacksmiths hammer points on the skewers
we use for cooking kabob. The sparks
delight the darkness of the anvil.
In woodshops, the boys
are nailing narrow slats on the crates.
Sweet-voiced Fairuz in the morning.
   I have loved you in summer
   I have loved you in winter
Salim at noon sings Ways of Ascent
a voice as pure as unblemished sky.
   From Allah the Lord of the Easts and the Wests

83

The East—Abu Kamal. My bus arrives,
empties its load in the brown blow.
Winter *khamsin*. The dust
obscures the sun-colored fruit of the mandarin stands.
Boys are hiding their faces from blowing sand,
driving their donkeys down the windy streets.
Again the smeared red strokes
dark arterial crude
on walls near the house of the friend
I have traveled to see, see DEATH
TO AMERICA and wonder again what America means.
To the hands that scrawled
DEATH TO AMERICA   America
what do you mean?

The West—the brown staked plains
of my white generations—they too wear
the veil of a dark dusty wind.
Sheep and cattle shielding themselves
with the meat of their own haunches. Men close
the gates. The storm whips the flags
of courthouse and café—
women work over heaping plates, work and flirt,
patriots muster for coffee, cigarettes, politics,
watching the world from their corner,
talking, laughing, eating DEATH
TO AMERICA. America, what do you mean?
What does DEATH TO AMERICA mean?

Can one wish death to the stubborn barns
to oak and arroyo
deer leaping fences
quail and jackrabbits
in ditches and draws
leathery men
skin soft to the grit and wind
dominoes guitars box scores tractors
the barber clipping hair
glow and sizzle of red hot iron
blacksmith machinist livery lathe
strap and buckle fire and steam
women washing teaching cutting cooking loving
fidgeting children in church on Sunday

84

boys fussing with ties they'd rather not wear
girls making milkshakes in the Dairy Queen?

Death to these things?
Death to mesas and wind-swept plains?
Death to my children, my wife, and me?

Dust shadows a cold, dry land
I lift a bride's veil only to see
a bloody face

DEATH TO AGGRESSION DEATH TO BOMBS
DEATH TO INJUSTICE DEATH TO GREED
DEATH TO EXILE AND DISPOSSESSION
DEATH TO PREJUDICE PARTIALITY PRIDE
DEATH TO A MIND OF US VS THEM
DEATH TO INVASION OCCUPATION WAR
DEATH TO BLINDNESS
DEATH TO IGNORANCE
DEATH TO BELIEVING MY LIFE MATTERS MORE

Aggression has only one face
Carnage has only one face
Hate has only one face
Love has only one face
The face is beaten and covered with blood

　　Abu Kamal Deir az-Zur Halab Bilad ash-Sham
　　All of Arabia covered in haze
　　Lubbock Lamesa Big Spring Texas
　　America blind in blood-red haze

I wander the dim and narrow lanes
I bear the wind of the dry *khamsin*

　　I swear by the Lord of the Ways of Ascent
　　I swear by the Lord of the Easts and the Wests

let the words be carved on every heart
let the words be painted on every wall
let the words be written in every tongue

　　DEATH TO AMERICA

write the letters
write the words
write in hot crimson strokes with my blood.

✿✿✿✿

Night secures the streets.
The settling dust discovers stars
above exhausted fields.
The roar of slogans, hot and red,
hushed in the shadow
of vigilant moon.
The hard-driven beasts,
unburdened, turn to stable and to rest.
The old to their suppers,
the young to careless intent
and laughing gossip, filling the hours,
bewildering love.
No map reveals the landscape lost
or gained in shifting wind,
the transfer of earth
from here to there.
In the jasmine night of Bayyada,
the sweet old sheikh pours tea.
In the western houses of Texas
it fills our cups.

Omnipresent

From this mountain—the western coast of Syria.
Once our ships came fat with rats
and soldiers, God's army marching inland,
swords sharp for faith and slaughter.

Today green shadows here, the fallen stones
of their fortress.
The sea air breathed into crevices,
cold from the keep and cistern.

Appearing suddenly as a wild goat
from the slope, old Alawi woman,
hair hidden beneath red cloth, red gypsy dress.
I think I remember
thinking she must live here
among the warrior ghosts. Chamomile in flower
brewed themselves into light all around.

We sat in the shade of a clever gate.
Part of the wall had fallen down.
She built a fire.
The kindling gave
itself to the blaze
like her laughter to the sweet sea air.

I think I remember
thinking how great a goddess is
who doesn't covet anybody's praise.

She spoke with smiles. Her hands smooth
as a child's handled the wood.
On her knuckles, letters, tattooed.
Somehow I understood her foreign words.

Food appeared,
a simple meal of honey and bread.
She sat across the fire.
I think I remember
thinking she must be
from the village nearby.

She fed me, and I slept beneath the tower
in the sad memory of war.
When I woke the fire was cold, and she was gone.
In the fresh Mediterranean air
the cold stone keep was overgrown.

Abu Kamal

Dawn.
Just after prayers.
The mother of Malek
milks the cow.

Strained, scalded, stirred
with sugar.
We drink the milk warm
with rice.

A child in a red dress
crosses a field
of brown stubble.

The wheat is stacked for threshing.

One morning.
All this.

Clearly life is an old woman
who only pretends
her sweetest words are secrets.

The Journey Keeps Me

I have never been to Cleveland,
Cuba, Anchorage, the Congo.
Celestial Damascus slips from sight,
the green steps never succeeding, neither horse
nor camel. Snows lie deep
in the clefts of mountains. Worlds,
whole galaxies I neither have nor will
all star beam milky way arriving reached
nor reach. Yet in my sleep
I sweat in rumpled clothes,
hope and hurried connections, night
in the still and stranded station
nowhere on the way to where
I never get to any way as if
I could possess some space,
belong somewhere,
finish the journey,
inhabit any corner of creation.

Al Khan

November brings the bees to my patio
Looking for a place to rest. They are welcome
To my kitchen near the evergreens, to the jam
Smeared on a plate by the open window.

Flowers are rare and nectar is in short supply.
I can provide you little, black-legged companion,
But such as it is, I offer you this inn.
Come rest your wings awhile, then fly.

Beit Allah

I am building a house of God in my mind.
Minarets and a crucifix.
The table of the ten words my altar.
I build without stone,
only the green leaves and bright flowers of my thoughts,
receiving Wisdom like rain,
receiving Love like sunlight.
My compassion is the mortar,
and the empty space is filled
with the serenity of Buddha.
A *mihrab* of hope within, without,
on every side, up and down, above, below,
in every direction that God is,
surrounding me as sky surrounds earth.
All will be welcome to worship here.
Enter through the door of praise.
No icons, rituals, or creed.
Come and pray with me
within the walls of wellbeing.
You can find this house always
wherever you go
just by looking.

Lone Star Sufi

Shah Naqshband appeared in Texas
in search of another self.

A fräulein served him streudel;
his beard fell like the Kaiser.
A roustabout smeared his body with sludge;
he grew black with a sticky ablution.
On the coast of Corpus, among the naked swimmers,
he swallowed an ocean of knowledge.
A peach of the Hill Country, full of sunlight,
confided the secret of sweetness.
Chased in a ghetto of Houston,
he wore fate as low as his britches.
The preachers they preached him
a sermon, and his robe became rags of Isa.
Un vaquero fed him a pepper,
he looked through the eyes of machismo.
He strung wire fence in the Valley,
biting the space between strands.
A cadaver of Austin read the veins of a leaf,
he beheld Bukhara on fire.
He spat out barbs, wrapped them in folly,
stitched his rags into patches aware as peaches,
wept oceans that washed the sludge from his pants,
his beard braided long as a river.

All this is true, and God was glad,
for he was himself again.

The Citadel

Nothing
mocks the fantasy of plans
like a walk around the Citadel.
  Every beggar opens hands
for a little now of love,
    voices
    circling this and that
    form doors on faces
shining out of black clothes
  like satellites
                half eclipsed
  in codes that seem to matter.
  Precious,
what matters is we here
together, forever on the way somewhere
  with crowds of moon-blessed creatures,
  lights golden on the old stones,
  cafés, shops, taxis, press
of pedestrians
  no less alive than Father Abraham
milking sheep,
storm god blowing in the night,
one night when you will say to me
  My daughter, every orbit carries
forward.
  Enough. More.
  The milky Aum of momentum will tell me
wherever you are
the meaning of your breath
  and why,
revealed by life,
  every word you spoke
rose up, miraculous, from the pavement
  to thrill my soul in the ancient air.
Dear friend,
what brought us to these ruins, side
by side,
  dreams in every siege of disappearing.
Let body hide
  in other bodies,
  you gave me something

small,
  perfect and invisible as pollen.
And it has grown.

GLOSSARY
of Arabic Words, Phrases, and Place Names

Transliterating Arabic into the English alphabet can be quite problematic. Because the method used in this collection avoids phonetic symbols, the Latin letters do not always correspond exactly to the Arabic letters and sounds. For example, the Latin letter *d* is used to represent two different letters in Arabic. The Arabic letter *ein* or *ayn*, a difficult sound for the native English speaker, is represented by an apostrophe. When the definite article *al* precedes one of the "sun letters," the *-l* is dropped and replaced by the following letter to indicate the doubling in pronunciation. Many of the Arabic words are those used in the Syrian dialect.

abu – father of; not a name in itself but often used with a son's name to refer to the father; for example, after the birth of his son Nadim, Ahmed might be referred to as Abu Nadim

adhan – call to prayer

ahlan – also *ahlan wa sahlan* or *ahla-wu-sahla*, a traditional phrase of greeting and welcome, meaning something like "you are among your family and have arrived on level ground" or roughly the equivalent of "make yourself at home and take it easy"

ahwe – coffee; *ahwe arabi* as typically served in Syria is strongly brewed from finely ground beans and served in demitasse cups

ajnabi – foreigner, alien; often the object of radical hospitality

Allah – God, generally understood as the one and only God, worshipped by all monotheistic believers; of course, specific theologies vary from religion to religion, believer to believer; One in Whose name no evil deed should ever be done

Allahu akbar – literally, "God is greater"; called *takbir*, the first two words of the *adhan* (call to prayers). This phrase reminds Muslims throughout their daily lives that God is much more worthy of attention and consideration than the trivialities of worldly life. Also it signifies that His mercy will be greater than all the sadness or hardship that one might experience. This phrase is used in *jihad* ("struggle") to express that no matter how powerful the enemy (whether Satan, temptation, a military force), God is more powerful. In common usage, this phrase is sometimes uttered to express amazement at something.

argheileh – a form of tobacco smoking using a large water pipe (*hookah*), once common in cafes and coffee shops throughout the Middle East; also called *nargheleh*, *shisha*, and hubble-bubble

97

Azizieh – predominantly Christian quarter of Aleppo, home to Arab Christians and to Armenians; welcomed by the Syrian government, many Armenians emigrated to Syria during the Turkish genocide

bab – door, gate

Bab Antakya – one of the ancient gates of Aleppo, defending the city against attacks from the west

Bab al Hadid – one of the ancient gates of Aleppo; the Iron Gate

Bab Qinnasrin – one of the ancient gates of Aleppo, a formidable defense

banjaan – eggplant

basal – onion

bass – enough, colloquial; sometimes used to refuse a fourth or fifth helping of *kibbe*

Bayyada – a quarter (neighborhood or section) in the Old City of Aleppo, located between the Citadel and Bab al Hadid

beit – house

Bilad ash-Sham – greater Syria, including present-day Syria as well as parts of Palestine, Jordan, Lebanon, Iraq, and Turkey; Sham is the classical Arabic name for Syria

boorj – tower

Dar al Islam – the territory (or world) of Islam; that is, those portions of the globe under Islamic rule, as opposed to *Dar al Harb*, the region of war, or the region where a Muslim cannot practice his/her religion safely

du'a – prayer or supplication to God, different from *salat*, the five formal prayers; to "make *du'a*" is to intercede or petition God directly

'Eid – feast or festival, often used as an abbreviation of 'Eid al Fitr, a holiday following Ramadan, the Muslims' month of fasting

emberha – colloquial word for yesterday

fatwa – opinion or ruling from a religious authority

fondoq – hotel

fustuq – pistachio, commodity for which Aleppo is well known

Gabal Mousa – the Mountain of Moses, Mount Sinai; here the Arabic letter *jiim* is transliterated to indicate pronunciation of *jabl* (mountain) in Egyptian dialect

Hadith – Hadith is Prophet Muhmmad's sayings and non-Quranic statements. Sometimes it refers to the Prophet's tradition as a whole including his actions and his tacit approvals (pbuh).

Hajji – one who has successfully completed the pilgrimage to Mecca (*hajj*)

Halab – Arabic name for Aleppo, Syria, which competes with Damascus for the title of oldest continuously inhabited city on earth; the Arabic name of the city may refer to the legend that Abraham milked (*halaba* = milk) his sheep on the large hill where the Citadel is now located

halal – Islamic term meaning lawful or acceptable

hammam – general term for bath and specifically for the old Turkish bath houses

haram – Islamic term meaning unlawful or forbidden

ibn – son

imam – leader of a mosque

in shaa'llah – literally, "if God wills"; an obligatory pronouncement when referring to the future

itfadel – a conventional term of politeness meaning "after you," often spoken in doorways and frequently repeated numerous times in fierce competitions of hospitality and politeness.

iwan – large arch or vaulted space used in Islamic architecture, often as entry to a mosque or courtyard

jaami' – another word for mosque (*masjid*); usually a jaami' is bigger than a mosque.

Jaami' ar-Rahman – a large mosque in Aleppo, Syria, near Sabeel Park

jabas – watermelon

jabl – mountain

Al Juma' – or Yom al Juma', Friday (literally, Day of Gathering), when most Muslims go to mosque for the noon prayer and message/speech by the *imam*

kaneesa – church

khalas – enough, finished

khamsin – a kind of sandstorm

khan – caravansarai

khubz – bread; the most common type of Arabic bread (*khubz arabi*) is a large, round, flat loaf, like pita bread, often broken into pieces and used for dipping food from a common serving dish

laban – yogurt

madrasa – school

masaa al khair – good evening; literally, "evening of goodness"; familiar Arabic greeting

masaa an nur – "evening of light"; the appropriate response to the greeting *masaa al khair*

al maseer – a hike or long walk. Father France, a Dutch priest and long-time resident in Syria, leads long walks several times a year in Syria; the strenuous hikes are completely ecumenical.

masjid – mosque

mihrab – niche inside a mosque which indicates the direction of Mecca, which believers face when praying

minaret – literally, "place of light (*nur*)"; mosque tower from which the muezzin calls believers to the daily prayers; originally used as watch towers

minbar – platform or pulpit from which the imam delivers messages and guidance to the believers

muezzin – person who calls the believers to the mosque for prayers

p.b.u.h. – abbreviation for "Peace be upon him," often written (or said) in English texts after mentioning the name of a prophet

qalb – heart; not to be confused with *kalb* (dog)

Ar-Rahman – the All-Compassionate or Most Gracious, one of the 99 beautiful names for God; also the title of a *sura* (chapter) of the Qur'an: "Of Him seeks (its need) every creature in the heavens and on earth: every day in (new) Splendour doth He (shine)! Then which of the favours of your Lord will ye deny?" (Al Qur'an 55: 29-30; Yusuf Ali translation)

rutab – an especially delectable date grown in Persia

sahn – courtyard; in mosque architecture, the *sahn* typically contains the ablution pool (*howz*) and is a place where believers gather to wash ceremonially before prayers

as-salaam aleikum – "peace be upon you," traditional Arabic greeting; the appropriate response is *wa leikum as-salaam*, "and upon you peace"

salat – one of the five daily ritual prayers in Islam

Salat al Fajr – the first of the five daily prayers. There is a span of time during which this prayer must be performed. The time spans starts at the arrival of the first thread of dawn light and ends by sunrise.

Salat al 'Isha – the last of the five daily prayers, performed at the arrival of complete darkness

service – pronounced ser-VEES; a small van or bus holding 10-12 people and used for cheap transportation

Shaitan – the adversary, Satan or the devil; one who rebelled against God; the whisperer

shari' – street or way

shari'a – Islamic law

sheikh – a respected elder or chief; often an honorific term, not an official position

shukran – thank you

subhan-Allahi wa bihamdihi – literally, "Glory [be] to God and praise to Him"; to utter this phrase is a blessed practice of benefit to the whole world

sunna – Islamic customs and traditions, especially rooted in the Qur'an and the teachings and sayings (*hadith*) of the Prophet Muhammad

suq – a shop, market

tannur – traditional oven

thum – garlic

ya'ni – a verbal filler, roughly equivalent to "it means"

zeit – olive oil, or simply oil in general

photo by Danny Meyer,
provided courtesy of Angelo State Unversity

About the Author

Chris Ellery, who has been a Fulbright lecturer at the University of Aleppo in Syria, has published short fiction and poetry in dozens of journals and literary magazines, including *Cimarron Review, Tar River Review, New Texas*, and *descant*. He has published two collections of poetry: *Quarry* and *All This Light We Live In*. His poem "Bimaristan Arghun" won the 2005 Betsy Colquitt Award, and in 2009 he was inducted into the Texas Institute of Letters.

With Asmahan Sallah he translated a collection of short stories, *Whatever Happened to Antara* (2004, the Center for Middle Eastern Studies, UT Austin) by award-winning Syrian author Walid Ikhlassi.

Ellery has visited Syria many times and has traveled extensively through-out the Middle East.

Currently he teaches American literature, film criticism and poetry writing at Angelo State University.

www.ingramcontent.com/pod-product-compliance
Lightning Source LLC
Chambersburg PA
CBHW020916090426
42736CB00008B/656